# AID ACROSS BORDERS

## Inside the $95 Billion Foreign Aid Package

**ETHAN REYNOLDS**

# TABLE OF CONTENTS


**INTRODUCTION** 7

**CHAPTER 1: THE GENESIS OF THE $95 BILLION AID PACKAGE** 11

Overview of the Aid Package and Its Significance 12

Background on the House and Senate Roles in Foreign Aid Legislation 13

Introduction to Key Players and Their Initial Positions 14

**CHAPTER 2: THE HOUSE'S PASSAGE AND THE SENATE'S PROCEDURAL VOTES** 15

The House's Passage of the Aid Package 15

Analysis of the Senate's Procedural Votes and Their Implications 16

Insights into the Legislative Process and Potential Challenges 17

**CHAPTER 3: UNITING FOUR BILLS: A COMPREHENSIVE AID PACKAGE** 19

Breakdown of the Four Bills 19

Allocation of Funds 20

Explanation of Sanctions on Russian Assets and TikTok Ban Language 21

**CHAPTER 4: HOUSE SPEAKER'S RESISTANCE AND BIPARTISAN SUPPORT** 23

House Speaker's Resistance 23

Bipartisan Support 24

Insights into the Political Dynamics and
Negotiations Involved   24

**CHAPTER 5: STALLED AID AND BORDER
SECURITY DEBATES**   **27**

Overview of the Delays in Aid for Ukraine and
Israel   27

Explanation of Republican Demands for Action
on Border Security   27

Details of the Negotiations and Eventual
Abandonment of a Border Package   28

**CHAPTER 6: SCHUMER'S AGREEMENT
AND SENATE'S RETURN FROM RECESS**   **31**

Chuck Schumer's Announcement of an
Agreement   31

Senate's Decision to Return from Recess and
Prioritize the Aid Package   32

Implications of the Senate's Actions on the
Timeline for Passing the Aid Package   32

**CHAPTER 7: ENSURING AID DELIVERY
AND GLOBAL IMPLICATIONS**   **35**

Schumer's Assurance of Aid Delivery   35

Analysis of Global Implications   36

Insights into the Importance of Foreign Aid in
Diplomatic Relations   37

**CONCLUSION AND FUTURE PROSPECTS**   **39**

Recap of the Aid Package's Journey through the
House and Senate   39

Discussion of the Potential Impact of the Aid
Package on International Relations   40

Reflections on the Importance of Foreign Aid in
Addressing Global Challenges          41

# INTRODUCTION

The genesis of the $95 billion aid package marks a significant milestone in U.S. foreign aid efforts, showcasing a comprehensive approach to addressing key global challenges. This aid package, aimed at providing crucial support to Ukraine, Israel, Taiwan, and the Indo-Pacific region, represents a coordinated effort by both the House and Senate to address pressing international needs. The House and Senate play crucial roles in shaping U.S. foreign aid policy. The House, as the lower chamber of Congress, has the power to initiate spending bills, including those related to foreign aid. The Senate, on the other hand, must approve these bills before they can become law. This process ensures that both chambers of Congress have a say in shaping foreign aid policy, reflecting the principles of checks and balances enshrined in the U.S. Constitution. Key players in the aid package's genesis include House Speaker Mike Johnson, who initially faced resistance within his own party regarding the aid package. Despite this, Speaker Johnson ultimately led the House in passing the aid package with broad bipartisan support. This bipartisan backing underscores the importance of foreign aid as a bipartisan issue, highlighting the shared commitment of lawmakers to address global challenges through diplomacy and aid.

The aid package's journey through the House and Senate was not without its challenges. The House's passage of the aid package was a crucial first step, demonstrating the House's commitment to supporting key allies and addressing critical needs in regions facing geopolitical challenges. The Senate's procedural votes further solidified support for the aid package, setting the stage for its final passage. The aid package combines four bills, each addressing specific needs and challenges. These bills allocate significant funds for Ukraine, Israel, Taiwan, and the Indo-Pacific region, reflecting the U.S. government's commitment to supporting these key allies and partners. Additionally, the aid package includes provisions for increased sanctions on Russian assets and language that could lead to a ban on TikTok in the U.S., demonstrating a multifaceted approach to addressing global challenges. The aid package's passage also highlights the importance of foreign aid in maintaining diplomatic relations and promoting stability. By ensuring aid delivery to key allies and partners, the U.S. can strengthen its global partnerships and promote peace and security. The aid package's global implications are far-reaching, demonstrating the U.S.'s commitment to addressing global challenges through diplomacy and aid. In conclusion, the $95 billion aid package represents a significant step forward in U.S. foreign aid policy, showcasing a comprehensive approach to addressing key global challenges. Its passage demonstrates the bipartisan support for foreign aid and underscores the importance of diplomacy in addressing global challenges. As the aid package moves forward, it is essential to reflect on its potential impact on international relations and the broader implications for global stability.

# CHAPTER 1: THE GENESIS OF THE $95 BILLION AID PACKAGE

In the swirling currents of global politics, aid often acts as a lifeboat for nations facing turbulent waters. The $95 billion aid package emerged as a beacon of hope amidst the storm clouds of uncertainty, aiming to provide much-needed assistance to Ukraine, Israel, and Taiwan. But how did this monumental aid package come to be?

At its core, the aid package represents a collaborative effort by lawmakers to address pressing international issues. It didn't materialize out of thin air; rather, it was born from a series of negotiations, compromises, and legislative maneuvers. The genesis of the aid package can be traced back to the recognition of the urgent need for support in key regions facing geopolitical challenges.

## Overview of the Aid Package and Its Significance

The aid package stands as a testament to the United States' commitment to global stability and security. With a staggering $95 billion allocated, it is one of the largest foreign aid packages in recent memory. This funding is not merely a gesture of goodwill; it serves as a lifeline for nations grappling with conflict, instability, and humanitarian crises.

At its core, the aid package addresses three primary areas of concern: Ukraine, Israel, and Taiwan. Each of these regions faces unique challenges, from military aggression to economic strain. By providing substantial financial assistance, the aid package aims to bolster the resilience of these nations and enhance their ability to navigate turbulent waters. Moreover, the aid package is not just about monetary support; it is also a symbol of solidarity and partnership. In extending a helping hand to nations in need, the United States reaffirms its role as a global leader and a beacon of hope for those facing adversity. In a world rife with uncertainty, the aid package sends a powerful message: that in times of crisis, we stand together as allies and friends.

## Background on the House and Senate Roles in Foreign Aid Legislation

To understand the journey of the aid package, it's essential to grasp the roles of the House and Senate in foreign aid legislation. The House of Representatives and the Senate play distinct yet complementary roles in shaping US foreign policy, including the allocation of aid.

In the House, lawmakers represent the diverse interests and perspectives of their constituents. Here, debates are lively, and negotiations are often fierce as representatives seek to advocate for the needs of their districts. The House is where the aid package took its first steps, with lawmakers deliberating over its scope, provisions, and funding allocations. Meanwhile, the Senate serves as a deliberative body, providing a forum for deeper examination and analysis of legislative proposals. Senators bring their expertise and experience to bear on complex issues, ensuring that legislation reflects the best interests of the nation as a whole. In the case of the aid package, the Senate's role was crucial in refining and fine-tuning the bill before its passage.

## Introduction to Key Players and Their Initial Positions

Every legislative journey is shaped by the individuals involved, and the aid package is no exception. From House Speaker Mike Johnson to Senate Majority Leader Chuck Schumer, key players have played pivotal roles in shaping the fate of the aid package. House Speaker Mike Johnson initially faced resistance from some quarters within his own party, who questioned the wisdom of providing aid to foreign nations. However, he ultimately rallied bipartisan support for the aid package, recognizing the importance of standing in solidarity with allies in times of need.

On the Senate side, Majority Leader Chuck Schumer emerged as a vocal advocate for the aid package, emphasizing the importance of delivering assistance to nations facing adversity. Schumer's leadership was instrumental in navigating the legislative process and overcoming obstacles to passage. As the aid package makes its way through the halls of Congress, these key players will continue to shape its trajectory, ensuring that it reaches its destination and fulfills its promise of support to nations in need.

# CHAPTER 2: THE HOUSE'S PASSAGE AND THE SENATE'S PROCEDURAL VOTES

## The House's Passage of the Aid Package

The $95 billion foreign aid package, aimed at providing aid to Ukraine, Israel, and Taiwan, passed the House of Representatives after months of deliberation and negotiation. The passage of this legislation was a significant step towards providing much-needed assistance to these countries and regions facing various challenges.

The House's passage of the aid package was a result of bipartisan cooperation and compromise. Lawmakers from both parties came together to support the legislation, recognizing the importance of providing aid to countries in need. The aid package, which combined four separate bills, allocated $61 billion for Ukraine, over $26 billion for Israel, and more than $8 billion for the Indo-Pacific region.

The House's passage of the aid package was not without its challenges. House Speaker Mike Johnson initially faced resistance from some members of his own party, who opposed sending aid to Ukraine. However, Johnson was able to navigate these challenges and secure broad bipartisan support for the legislation.

## Analysis of the Senate's Procedural Votes and Their Implications

After passing the House, the aid package moved to the Senate, where it faced additional hurdles. The Senate began the process with two procedural votes, which were crucial steps in advancing the legislation towards a final vote.

The procedural votes in the Senate were an important part of the legislative process. These votes helped determine the timeline for consideration of the aid package and allowed senators to express their support or opposition to the legislation. While the Senate was expected to have enough support from both parties to pass the legislation, the exact timing for a final vote remain uncertain. The implications of the Senate's procedural votes were significant. A successful outcome would mean that the aid package could move forward to a final vote and potentially be signed into law by President Joe Biden. However, any delay or obstruction could prolong the process and jeopardize the timely delivery of aid to Ukraine, Israel, and Taiwan.

## Insights into the Legislative Process and Potential Challenges

The legislative process for passing the $95 billion aid package highlighted the complexities of lawmaking in Congress. The process involved multiple stages, including committee hearings, floor debates, and votes in both the House and Senate. Lawmakers had to navigate competing interests and priorities to reach a consensus on the aid package.

One of the key challenges faced during the legislative process was the need to balance the allocation of funds among different countries and regions. Lawmakers had to weigh the needs of Ukraine, Israel, and Taiwan against other priorities and considerations, such as budget constraints and geopolitical considerations. Another challenge was the need to address concerns raised by members of Congress and other stakeholders. Some lawmakers expressed reservations about certain aspects of the aid package, such as the inclusion of sanctions on Russian assets and language that could lead to a ban on TikTok in the US. These concerns had to be addressed through negotiations and amendments to the legislation.

Overall, the passage of the $95 billion aid package through the House and Senate was a testament to the bipartisan cooperation and commitment to providing aid to countries and regions in need. The legislative process was complex and challenging, but ultimately successful in advancing the aid package towards final passage.

# CHAPTER 3: UNITING FOUR BILLS: A COMPREHENSIVE AID PACKAGE

The $95 billion foreign aid package is a combination of four separate bills that were previously voted on individually by the House. This comprehensive package aims to provide aid to Ukraine, Israel, Taiwan, and the Indo-Pacific region, while also including provisions for sanctions on Russian assets and language that could lead to a ban on TikTok in the US.

## Breakdown of the Four Bills

The first bill in the aid package provides nearly $61 billion in aid for Ukraine. This includes military assistance to help Ukraine defend itself against Russian aggression, as well as humanitarian aid to support the Ukrainian people who have been affected by the conflict. The second bill allocates over $26 billion in aid for Israel. This includes funding for Israel's Iron Dome missile defense system, which has been crucial in protecting Israeli civilians from missile attacks.

The third bill provides more than $8 billion in aid for the Indo-Pacific region. This includes funding for programs to promote democracy, human rights, and economic development in countries like Taiwan, Vietnam, and the Philippines.

The fourth bill in the aid package focuses on increasing sanctions on Russian assets. It includes provisions that could lead to a ban on TikTok in the US if its parent company, ByteDance, does not sell the app within nine months.

## Allocation of Funds

The aid package allocates funds based on the specific needs of each region. For example, Ukraine receives a significant amount of military aid due to its ongoing conflict with Russia, while Israel receives funding for its missile defense system to protect against threats from groups like Hamas and Hezbollah. In the Indo-Pacific region, the aid is aimed at promoting stability and economic development. This includes funding for programs that help countries in the region strengthen their democratic institutions and improve their economies.

## Explanation of Sanctions on Russian Assets and TikTok Ban Language

The inclusion of sanctions on Russian assets is a response to Russia's aggression in Ukraine and its interference in other countries' affairs. These sanctions are designed to put pressure on Russia to change its behavior and respect international norms. The language regarding a potential ban on TikTok in the US is part of the ongoing concern over the app's ties to China and the potential security risks it poses. By giving ByteDance nine months to sell TikTok, the US government is seeking to address these security concerns and protect American users' data.

In conclusion, the $95 billion foreign aid package represents a comprehensive effort to provide aid to countries in need while also addressing security and geopolitical concerns. It reflects a bipartisan commitment to supporting allies and promoting stability and democracy around the world.

# CHAPTER 4: HOUSE SPEAKER'S RESISTANCE AND BIPARTISAN SUPPORT

## House Speaker's Resistance

House Speaker Mike Johnson initially resisted bringing the aid package to the floor for a vote. This resistance stemmed from various factors, including concerns about the size of the package, its specific provisions, and potential political ramifications. Johnson, like many other politicians, had to weigh the benefits of providing aid to Ukraine, Israel, and Taiwan against potential criticism or backlash from constituents or fellow party members.

Johnson's resistance was also influenced by broader political considerations. As a leader within the Republican Party, Johnson had to balance the demands of different factions within his party. Some Republicans were opposed to providing aid to Ukraine and other countries, viewing it as unnecessary or potentially detrimental to American interests. Johnson had to navigate these internal party dynamics while also considering the broader implications of the aid package for foreign policy and international relations.

## Bipartisan Support

Despite initial resistance, the aid package ultimately received broad bipartisan support in the House. This bipartisan backing was crucial for the package's passage, as it ensured that it would not be derailed by partisan politics. Members of both parties recognized the importance of providing aid to Ukraine, Israel, and Taiwan, and were willing to set aside their differences to support the package.

The bipartisan support for the aid package was a reflection of the broader consensus on foreign aid within Congress. While there may have been disagreements on specific provisions or funding levels, there was a general understanding among lawmakers that providing aid to countries facing security or humanitarian challenges was in the best interests of the United States. This bipartisan consensus helped to overcome any lingering resistance to the aid package and paved the way for its passage.

## Insights into the Political Dynamics and Negotiations Involved

The House Speaker's initial resistance and the eventual bipartisan support for the aid package highlight the complex political dynamics at play in foreign aid legislation. Lawmakers must balance competing interests and priorities, both within their own party and across party lines, while also considering the broader implications of their decisions for foreign policy and international relations. Negotiations over the aid package likely involved discussions about the specific allocations for Ukraine, Israel, and Taiwan, as well as the inclusion of sanctions on Russian assets and language related to TikTok. Lawmakers may have also debated the timing of the aid package and its relationship to other legislative priorities, such as border security. Overall, the House Speaker's resistance and the bipartisan support for the aid package underscore the importance of diplomacy and negotiation in the legislative process. While there may be disagreements and challenges along the way, lawmakers ultimately came together to support a package that they believed would further American interests and values on the global stage.

# CHAPTER 5: STALLED AID AND BORDER SECURITY DEBATES

## Overview of the Delays in Aid for Ukraine and Israel

The process of providing aid to Ukraine and Israel hit a roadblock due to debates over border security. Both Democrats and Republicans in Congress agreed on the importance of aid to these countries, but they couldn't reach a consensus on the timing and conditions for providing this aid.

The delays in aid for Ukraine and Israel were mainly caused by disagreements over whether to address border security issues before allocating funds for foreign aid. Some Republicans argued that securing the border should be a top priority, especially in light of ongoing security challenges.

## Explanation of Republican Demands for Action on Border Security

Republicans in Congress demanded action on border security as a condition for supporting the aid package. They argued that securing the border was essential for national security and that addressing border issues should take precedence over other legislative priorities. Republicans also raised concerns about the potential for increased immigration and security risks if border security measures were not addressed. They believed that providing aid to Ukraine and Israel should be contingent on addressing these security concerns.

## Details of the Negotiations and Eventual Abandonment of a Border Package

Negotiations between Democrats and Republicans on a border security package tied to foreign aid lasted for months but ultimately failed. Democrats were willing to consider some border security measures but were reluctant to make them a condition for providing aid to Ukraine and Israel.

Despite efforts to find a compromise, the negotiations eventually collapsed, leading to the abandonment of the border package. This meant that aid for Ukraine and Israel remained stalled, as Republicans refused to support the aid package without action on border security.

In the end, the aid package was passed separately from any border security measures, highlighting the challenges of reaching bipartisan agreement on complex issues like foreign aid and border security.

Overall, the delays in providing aid to Ukraine and Israel underscored the challenges of navigating partisan politics and legislative priorities in Congress. While both parties agreed on the importance of providing aid to these countries, they struggled to find common ground on the conditions for providing this aid, leading to months of negotiations and eventual abandonment of a border security package.

# CHAPTER 6: SCHUMER'S AGREEMENT AND SENATE'S RETURN FROM RECESS

## Chuck Schumer's Announcement of an Agreement

Chuck Schumer, the Senate Majority Leader, made a significant announcement regarding the $95 billion foreign aid package. After months of negotiations and delays, Schumer declared that an agreement had been reached to complete work on the aid package. This announcement marked a crucial step forward in the legislative process, bringing the aid package closer to final approval.

Schumer's announcement was met with both relief and anticipation. The aid package, aimed at providing crucial assistance to Ukraine, Israel, and Taiwan, had been a subject of intense debate and scrutiny. Schumer's ability to secure an agreement was seen as a testament to his leadership and negotiation skills.

## Senate's Decision to Return from Recess and Prioritize the Aid Package

In a surprising move, the Senate decided to interrupt its scheduled recess to address the aid package. This decision underscored the importance of the aid package and the Senate's commitment to passing it in a timely manner. Despite the Passover holiday, senators agreed to return to Washington to focus on the aid package, demonstrating a sense of urgency and dedication to the issue.

The decision to prioritize the aid package over other legislative matters was not taken lightly. Senators recognized the significance of the aid package, not just for the countries receiving aid but also for the broader geopolitical landscape. By returning from recess, the Senate signaled its determination to see the aid package through to completion.

## Implications of the Senate's Actions on the Timeline for Passing the Aid Package

The Senate's actions had immediate implications for the timeline of passing the aid package. By interrupting recess and prioritizing the aid package, senators aimed to expedite the legislative process and ensure timely delivery of aid to Ukraine, Israel, and Taiwan.

The first vote on the aid package was scheduled for Tuesday afternoon, with the final vote expected no later than Wednesday night. This timeline was ambitious but achievable, thanks to the Senate's commitment to swift action.

The Senate's actions also sent a strong message to the international community. By prioritizing foreign aid, especially in the midst of a holiday recess, the Senate demonstrated its solidarity with countries in need and its determination to uphold America's commitments on the global stage.

In conclusion, Schumer's announcement of an agreement to finish work on the aid package, coupled with the Senate's decision to return from recess and prioritize the aid package, had significant implications for the legislative process. The Senate's actions reflected a sense of urgency and determination to pass the aid package and deliver much-needed assistance to Ukraine, Israel, and Taiwan.

# CHAPTER 7: ENSURING AID DELIVERY AND GLOBAL IMPLICATIONS

In the tumultuous landscape of global politics, aid plays a pivotal role in providing stability and support to nations in need. The recent $95 billion foreign aid package passed by the House and under consideration by the Senate is a testament to the commitment of the United States to extend a helping hand to its allies and partners across the world. Senate Majority Leader Chuck Schumer's assurance of aid delivery to Ukraine, NATO allies, Israel, and others underscores the importance of this aid package in addressing pressing global challenges.

## Schumer's Assurance of Aid Delivery

Senator Schumer's assurance of aid delivery is a crucial reassurance to nations facing geopolitical turmoil. For Ukraine, embroiled in a conflict with Russia, this aid is a lifeline that strengthens its ability to defend its sovereignty and protect its citizens. The aid package includes substantial funding to support Ukraine's military capabilities, humanitarian assistance, and economic development. This support is not just about financial aid but also about showing solidarity and commitment to democratic values.

NATO allies, particularly those in Eastern Europe, also benefit from this aid package. It reaffirms the United States' commitment to the NATO alliance and helps bolster the defense capabilities of these nations, enhancing regional security and deterring aggression. Israel, a longstanding ally in the Middle East, receives significant aid to support its defense and security needs. This aid package reinforces the strong bond between the United States and Israel, highlighting America's commitment to Israel's security and stability in a volatile region.

## Analysis of Global Implications

The passage of the aid package has far-reaching implications beyond the immediate beneficiaries. It sends a clear message to the international community about the United States' stance on key global issues. By providing substantial aid to Ukraine, the United States demonstrates its support for countries facing aggression and its commitment to upholding international law and sovereignty.

The aid package also reflects the United States' strategic interests in the Indo-Pacific region. With over $8 billion allocated for the Indo-Pacific, the aid package aims to bolster partnerships and counter the influence of authoritarian regimes in the region. This demonstrates America's commitment to maintaining a free and open Indo-Pacific, which is crucial for regional stability and prosperity.

## Insights into the Importance of Foreign Aid in Diplomatic Relations

Foreign aid is not just about providing financial assistance; it is also a powerful tool of diplomacy. It allows nations to build and strengthen relationships, promote peace, and address global challenges collectively. By providing aid to countries like Ukraine, Israel, and others, the United States not only supports their development but also fosters goodwill and strengthens diplomatic ties. In conclusion, the $95 billion foreign aid package represents a significant commitment by the United States to support its allies and partners in times of need. Senator Schumer's assurance of aid delivery underscores the importance of this aid package in addressing global challenges and maintaining diplomatic relations. The implications of this aid package extend far beyond the financial support it provides, signaling America's commitment to peace, stability, and democracy around the world.

# CONCLUSION AND FUTURE PROSPECTS

## Recap of the Aid Package's Journey through the House and Senate

The $95 billion foreign aid package has been a journey marked by cooperation, negotiation, and bipartisan support. It started in the House, where lawmakers faced the challenge of combining four separate bills into one comprehensive package. This was no easy feat, as each bill had its own set of priorities and funding allocations.

House Speaker Mike Johnson initially resisted bringing the aid package to the floor, but eventually, bipartisan support prevailed, and the package passed with a strong majority. This was a significant moment, as it showed that even in a politically divided climate, lawmakers could come together to support crucial foreign aid initiatives.

The aid package then moved to the Senate, where it faced its own set of challenges. Procedural votes were required, and negotiations had to take place to ensure that the package would pass smoothly.

Senate Majority Leader Chuck Schumer played a key role in shepherding the package through the Senate, ultimately leading to a final vote that is expected to pass by midweek.

## Discussion of the Potential Impact of the Aid Package on International Relations

The passage of the aid package has the potential to have a significant impact on international relations. For Ukraine, Israel, and Taiwan, the aid represents a commitment from the United States to support their security and well-being. It sends a message to these countries and others around the world that the U.S. stands with them in times of need.

The inclusion of increased sanctions on Russian assets and language that could lead to a ban on TikTok in the U.S. also has broader implications. It shows that the U.S. is willing to take a strong stance against countries and companies that threaten its interests. This could have ripple effects in the international community, shaping how other countries perceive and interact with the U.S. on diplomatic and economic fronts.

# Reflections on the Importance of Foreign Aid in Addressing Global Challenges

Foreign aid plays a crucial role in addressing global challenges. It provides much-needed support to countries facing crises such as conflict, natural disasters, and economic instability. In the case of Ukraine, Israel, and Taiwan, the aid package is a lifeline that will help these countries defend themselves against external threats.

But foreign aid is not just about providing financial support. It is also about building relationships and promoting stability around the world. By supporting countries in need, the U.S. can help prevent conflicts from escalating and promote peace and prosperity.

In conclusion, the $95 billion foreign aid package represents a significant commitment from the U.S. to support its allies and address global challenges. It is a testament to the power of diplomacy and cooperation in tackling complex international issues. As the package moves forward, it is important to remember the impact it will have on the countries and people it is intended to help, and the broader implications it will have on international relations.

www.ingramcontent.com/pod-product-compliance
Lightning Source LLC
Chambersburg PA
CBHW051857250726
48659CB00006B/2253